C O N T E M P O R A R Y ' S

Breakthroughs

in Critical Reading

C O N T E M P O R A R Y ' S

Breakthroughs
in Critical Reading

EXERCISE BOOK

CØB

CONTEMPORARY BOOKS

a division of NTC/CONTEMPORARY PUBLISHING GROUP
Lincolnwood, Illinois USA

Acknowledgements

Cartoon on page 22, "For Better or For Worse," copyright © 1991 by Lynn Johnston Prod., Inc. Reprinted by permission of Universal Press Syndicate. All rights reserved.

Excerpt on page 26 from *Chicano* by Richard Vasquez. Copyright © 1970 by Richard Vasquez.

Poem on page 38, "I, Too, Sing America," from *Selected Poems* by Langston Hughes. Copyright © 1926 by Alfred A. Knopf, Inc. and renewed 1954 by Langston Hughes. Reprinted by permission of the publisher.

Play excerpt on page 40 from *The Odd Couple* by Neil Simon. Copyright © 1966 and renewed 1994 by Neil Simon. Reprinted by permission of Random House, Inc.

"Gojo Bridge in Kyoto" on page 52 from *Folk Legends of Japan* by Richard M. Dorson. Copyright © 1962 in Japan by Charles E. Tuttle Company, Inc. Reprinted by permission of the publisher.

Cartoon on page 53, "Beetle Bailey," by Mort Walker. Copyright © 1992 by King Features Syndicate, Inc. Reprinted by special permission of King Features Syndicate, Inc.

Poem on page 55, "Inventory," copyright © 1926, renewed 1954, by Dorothy Parker, from *The Portable Dorothy Parker* by Dorothy Parker, introduction by Brendan Gill. Used by permission of Viking Penguin, a division of Penguin Books USA Inc.

"The Game is Over" on page 56 from *Dandil: Stories from Iranian Life* by Gholam-Hossein Sa'Edi. Copyright © 1981 by Gholam-Hossein Sa'Edi. Reprinted by permission of Random House, Inc.

Play excerpt on page 58 from *I Never Sang for My Father* by Robert Anderson. Copyright © 1968 by Robert Anderson. Reprinted by permission of International Creative Management.

The editor has made every effort to trace the ownership of all copyrighted material, and necessary permissions have been secured in most cases. Should there prove to be any question regarding the use of any material, regret is hereby expressed for such error. Upon notification of any such oversight, proper acknowledgement will be made in future editions.

ISBN: 0-8092-3297-9

TO THE STUDENT

Welcome to *Breakthroughs in Critical Reading Exercise Book.* In this book, you'll be practicing the skills you learned in Contemporary's *Breakthroughs in Critical Reading* student book. You will practice how to read passages as well as cartoons, poetry, reviews, advertisements, and drama.

Each exercise in this book corresponds to one or more lessons in Breakthroughs in *Critical Reading.* Look for the page numbers under "Text Pages" in the margin of each exercise. They will tell you where to learn more about that skill in the *Breakthroughs* book.

You'll find answers to all the exercises at the back of the book. Be sure to check your work at the end of each exercise before you move on. The thinking-skill questions can be written on a separate piece of paper. Answer each question fully in your own words. Writing is a very important part of learning. Don't worry about your handwriting, grammar, or spelling at first. Concentrate on getting your ideas on paper.

When you are finished with the book, take the Post-Test. A chart on page 64 will help you evaluate the work you have done.

And finally, read beyond the pages of this book. Read newspapers, magazines, road maps, and anything else you might be interested in. Reading will help you prepare not only for academic study but also for the rest of your life.

UNDERSTANDING WHAT YOU READ

TEXT PAGES
13–16

Main Idea and Details

When you read, look for the main idea of the text. Often the main idea is directly stated in a sentence. Details give specific information about the main idea.

Directions: Read the passage, then answer the questions that follow.

Buffalo Snacks

Making a movie sometimes involves using certain tricks to get performing animals to do what is wanted. Animals don't understand directions the way people do. So they have to be directed in whatever way works.

The makers of the western film *Dances with Wolves* faced a special problem. They wanted to have a buffalo charge during a hunting scene. The challenge was to get the buffalo to charge on cue and in the right direction. A buffalo will charge when angry, but an angry buffalo would be too hard for the crew to control. It could also be dangerous. An accident might happen. Either the animal or the crew members might get hurt. The filmmakers had to think of a safe way to film the scene.

The problem was solved when someone located a buffalo that would do anything for his favorite food. The buffalo learned that if he ran forward when commanded, he would be rewarded with his favorite snack. In the dramatic scene in the movie where the buffalo seems to be charging in anger, he is not really attacking a young Sioux hunter. Actually, he is running at full speed toward a huge stack of Oreo cookies!

---

1. What is the main idea of the entire passage?

   (1) Animals don't understand directions the way people do.

   (2) The makers of the western film *Dances with Wolves* faced a special problem.

   (3) An accident might happen.

   (4) Making a movie sometimes involves using certain tricks to get performing animals to do what is wanted.

   (5) Actually, he is running at full speed toward a huge stack of Oreo cookies!

2. What is the main idea of the last paragraph in the passage?

(1) The problem was solved when someone located a buffalo that would do anything for his favorite food.

(2) The buffalo ran forward when commanded to do so.

(3) The buffalo seems to be charging in anger.

(4) The buffalo is not really attacking a young Sioux hunter.

(5) The buffalo is running toward a stack of Oreo cookies.

3. Match the item on the left with its description on the right. Write the matching letter on each line.

1. ____ buffalo		**a.** the kind of movie
2. ____ in a safe way		**b.** the name of the movie
3. ____ charge on cue		**c.** the kind of animal
4. ____ *Dances with Wolves*		**d.** what the animal is supposed to do
5. ____ Oreo cookies		**e.** the kind of scene the buffalo was to appear in
6. ____ western		**f.** how the crew wanted the scene to be filmed
7. ____ hunting		**g.** the buffalo's snack

THINKING SKILL

4. What did the makers of the movie want to avoid when getting the buffalo to charge?

Check your answers on page 67.

3

Main Ideas in Newspaper Articles

A newspaper reporter often develops a story with details that tell *who* and *what* the article is about, *where* and *when* the action happened, and *how* it happened. The main idea is often stated in the article's headline.

Directions: Read the newspaper article, then answer the questions that follow.

Heroine Thinks Press Too Pushy

Lynn Hawk, the schoolteacher who helped rescue students from a flash flood, feels that reporters can go too far. Hawk found herself in the public eye after she and her class narrowly escaped a sudden flood. They had been on a nature hike at Little Canyon on May 14 when a heavy rain caused the canyon river to overflow. Despite the danger, Hawk kept her students calm. The bus driver also helped keep the group together. All were led to safety. What worries Hawk now is the way the story was covered.

Hawk thinks the press was too pushy about getting the story. According to her, the reporters and TV camera crews at the scene of the incident seemed more concerned about the camera angle than about the victims. Hawk also thinks they should not have bothered her or the students at the hospital. All were too shaken to be questioned.

Even at home, Hawk says, the press wouldn't leave her alone. She had to get a relative to help with answering all the phone calls. They had trouble refusing newspaper requests for a photo. Hawk says the reporters wouldn't take a simple no for an answer.

Being publicly called a heroine also bothers Hawk. She thinks anyone would have done what she did. She feels that more credit should have been given to the bus driver. Hawk understands that the incident was newsworthy. But she thinks the press should have more respect for people's privacy.

---

1. What is the main idea of the newspaper article?

(1) The heroine thinks the press should be less aggressive.

(2) The teacher feels reporters don't go far enough.

(3) Camera crews are concerned only about their camera angles.

(4) Flash floods are big news.

2. The newspaper article did *not* give details about

    (1) the flash flood incident

    (2) the newspaper reports

    (3) what happened after the incident

    (4) how the teacher reacted

3. Match the questions on the left with the details from the article on the right. Write the matching letter on each line.

____ **(1)** Who is the heroine?

____ **(2)** What incident got in the news?

____ **(3)** When did it happen?

____ **(4)** Where did it happen?

____ **(5)** Where did the victims go after the incident?

____ **(6)** How did the press treat the teacher?

____ **(7)** What did the newspaper want?

____ **(8)** Who was ignored by the press?

    a. like a heroine

    b. to the hospital

    c. the bus driver

    d. the teacher, Lynn Hawk

    e. Little Canyon

    f. photos

    g. in May

    h. a rescue from a flash flood

4. What two types of news teams covered the incident?

_____

THINKING SKILL

5. Based on the article, how do you think Hawk wishes the reporters had acted?

Check your answers on page 67.

Unstated Main Ideas

Sometimes the main idea is not directly stated, and you must use the details to figure out the main idea.

Directions: Read the passage, then answer the questions that follow.

Zipper Up!

We take zippers for granted. But if it weren't for Whitcomb Judson, we might still need buttonhooks to fasten our boots. In 1893, this American engineer invented the zipper to replace boot buttons.

Buttons are useful for some clothing. They look good on blouses and other garments, serving as decoration as well as a closing device.

But buttoning up can't be done in a hurry. It has to be done one button at a time. And if the first button goes in the wrong hole, you have to start all over. The zipper is much quicker.

Judson's invention was based on the hook-and-eye system. A movable slide linked together a row of individual hooks that were sewn on a tape. The design made it possible for the opening or closing to be done in one movement. But the hooks tended to pop open. One of Judson's workers came up with an improvement. He replaced the hooks with teeth that locked tightly together.

By World War I, the zipper had been refined enough to use on clothing. U.S. pilots went to war wearing flight suits that fastened quickly and easily. Zippers worked so well that B. F. Goodrich started putting them on rubber boots in 1923. Now we find zippers on almost all our clothes. Jackets are securely closed. Pants and dresses fasten in a flash.

The next time you are zipping up in a hurry, say thanks to Mr. Judson. Remember the words of the 1926 salesman who gave the device its name. When he gave demonstrations, he would say, "Zip—it's open, zip—it's closed!"

---

1. Which of the following is the best title for the passage?

    (1) The Problem with Buttons

    (2) Military Uses of the Zipper

    (3) An American Inventor

    (4) The Great Fastener War

    (5) A Short History of the Zipper

2. Match the question on the left with the detail from the passage on the right. Write the matching letter on each line.

1. ____ When was the zipper invented?

2. ____ What did the zipper replace on boots?

3. ____ On what is the design of the zipper based?

4. ____ How were zippers improved?

5. ____ How were zippers used in World War I?

6. ____ Who used zippers to fasten rubber boots?

7. ____ Where can you find zippers today?

a. the hook-and-eye system

b. to fasten flight suits

c. on almost all of our clothes

d. B.F. Goodrich

e. in 1893

f. teeth replaced hooks

g. buttons

3. Fill in the blanks with the word or words from the passage that best complete the sentence.

a. Buttons are _____ for some clothing.

b. A _____ brings the teeth on a zipper together.

c. The zipper was named by a _____.

d. One problem with the early zipper was that it _____.

e. One reason why the zipper has become so popular is that it

_____.

f. Another reason why the zipper has become so popular is that it

_____.

THINKING SKILL 4. What does the author mean by saying you should thank Mr. Judson?

Check your answers on page 67.

Main Idea and Supporting Ideas

Details of a passage can be divided into two categories: general and specific. General details are called **supporting ideas.** These ideas explain the main idea in more depth. Specific details further develop and reinforce the supporting ideas by giving particular examples, reasons, definitions, or characteristics.

A Question of Money

There may come a time when you, like many people, will need a lawyer. One thing that you'll wonder is how much a good lawyer will cost. Remember that you are the customer. The attorney is selling a service. To get the best deal for your money when looking for a lawyer, find out about the different types of fees.

The most common way lawyers charge is by the hour. An hourly fee is based on how many hours the lawyer spends on your case. If a lawyer works 10 hours for you and charges $75 an hour, your bill will be $750.

Flat fees often are charged for routine legal matters. The most common place to find flat-fee rates is at a legal clinic.

A flat fee is a set total for the job done. For example, a lawyer might offer to write up your uncontested divorce for a set fee. The case should be simple because both people involved in the case are in agreement. No matter how many hours are spent on your case, all you pay is the set—or flat—fee. Sometimes with flat fees, you also have to agree to pay for typing and photocopying. Remember to ask what extra charges there might be.

Some cases, such as personal injury suits, are billed on a contingency basis. The payment depends on whether you win or lose the case. A lawyer bills this way when the client will not be able to pay for costs unless the case is won and the client receives damages. If the client wins, the lawyer charges an agreed percentage of what the judge awards. The percentage can range from 25 percent to 40 percent of the damages the client receives. If the client loses, he or she usually pays the lawyer nothing or a specified amount of basic expenses.

Whichever fee arrangement seems to fit your problem, be sure to shop around. Not all lawyers charge the same fees for a specific service. When you find a lawyer who suits your needs and your pocketbook, be sure to get a written agreement about the fee.

1. What is the main idea of the article?

_____

_____

_____

2. Which of the following are supporting ideas? **You may choose more than one.**

_____ **a.** Almost everyone needs to consult a lawyer sometime.

_____ **b.** Many lawyers charge by the hour.

_____ **c.** An uncontested divorce might be handled for a flat fee.

_____ **d.** Some cases are billed on a contingency basis.

3. Match each supporting idea on the left with its definition on the right. Write the matching letter on each line.

_____ **(1)** hourly fee

_____ **(2)** flat fee

_____ **(3)** contingency fee

    a. a set total for routine legal matters

    b. payment for every hour worked

    c. payment based on whether you win or lose

4. What example is given about hourly charges?

_____

_____

5. What example is given about flat fees?

_____

_____

_____

6. When does a lawyer bill a client on a contingency basis?

_____

_____

THINKING SKILL 7. What supporting idea gives advice about all three types of legal fees?

Check your answers on pages 67–68.

9

Summarizing a Passage _____

When you summarize, you tell the main idea and the important details in your own words.

Directions: Read the passage, then answer the questions that follow.

A Day in the Life

Dear Edith,

I promised to tell you if anything exciting ever happened out here. Well, the phone hasn't rung. No interesting people have come to visit. But yesterday proved the old proverb "trouble comes in threes."

The first thing I heard when I woke up was the sound of rushing water. My house is nowhere near a river or an ocean, so I knew something was wrong. I tracked the roar to the toilet tank in the bathroom. The thingamabob in the tank that controls the flow of water had stopped controlling anything. It was like Niagara Falls. All I could think of was how my water bill was getting bigger by the minute!

Having decided to go buy whatever gizmo would fix the problem, I went to check the mail. I stood on my porch trying to figure out what looked wrong. Something was missing. After a few blinks, I realized the mailbox was gone. Its little post stood there looking quite silly by itself. Apparently, kids out here get their Halloween kicks by swiping mailboxes. So I had another item to buy in town.

When I went to town, I found a sale on bathroom fixtures and basic metal mailboxes. So far, so good. I should have known better. On my way home, I heard an awful noise. Yes, the noise was coming from my car. Then there was a clunk, clunk! Would you believe my muffler had fallen off? Luckily, a muffler repair place is located at the edge of town. My car made a terrible noise for two blocks. It could have been heard in the next county! But no police officer stopped me. Then I got to sit for several hours while my muffler was replaced. I also got to shell out more money than I wanted.

So what do you think of country living now, Edith? Is it as carefree as you thought? A 10-mile trip for repairs can be a bit much. Just wait for the next letter. We are expecting a tornado soon.

Until next time, love ya,

Ann

---

1. To whom did the events in the letter happen?

   _____

2. Where does the person live?

   _____

3. To whom is the letter addressed?

   _____

4. When did the events take place?

   _____

5. Write the order in which each problem happened. Write *first, second,* and *third* on the lines.

   _____ **a.** the muffler

   _____ **b.** the toilet tank

   _____ **c.** the mailbox

6. Which paragraph best summarizes the passage?

   (1) Ann has written to Edith about three problems that happened in one day. Ann's toilet was broken and her mailbox was stolen. After she had gone into town for replacement parts, her muffler fell off. She had to spend a lot of money that day.

   (2) Ann promised to tell Edith if anything exciting ever happened to her while she was living away from the city. The phone didn't ring and no one came to visit. But she mentioned that a tornado was expected soon.

7. Which proverb best summarizes the ideas in the passage?

   (1) A stitch in time saves nine.

   (2) Absence makes the heart grow fonder.

   (3) A friend in need is a friend indeed.

   (4) When it rains, it pours.

   (5) Every cloud has a silver lining.

THINKING SKILL 8. What kind of relationship do you think Edith and Ann have? Are they good friends or business partners? Why do you think as you do?

Check your answers on page 68.

ORGANIZATION OF IDEAS

TEXT PAGES
56–61

Cause and Effect in Sentences

When one thing makes another thing happen, we call it a cause-and-effect relationship. The cause is what makes something happen. What happens as a result is the effect. Some key words that signal cause-and-effect relationships are *because, so, therefore, but, as a result, since, consequently, if . . . then, accordingly, this led to,* and *thus.*

Directions: Read the newspaper article, then answer the questions.

Mother Nature Reveals Human Nature

On Tuesday evening of last week, a tornado whipped through Marion, Illinois. The storm caused serious damage. But the tragedy also brought out the good side of many people.

Over 40 families lost their homes because of the 100-mile-an-hour winds. Pieces of their houses flew as far as four blocks away. At least 20 other families will need to replace items of furniture and parts of their houses due to damage done by flying bricks, wood, and glass. Rain also ruined many personal items. Because of damaged power lines, residents spent days without electricity.

A week later, another effect of the tornado could be seen. In the days that followed the storm, hundreds of people from Marion and the surrounding area made an effort to help out by donating food and clothing to the many families who had lost all their belongings.

As a result of the town's involvement, thousands of items of clothing were donated to Red Cross centers. Because of food donations, displaced families had plenty to eat. Because a local church donated its kitchen space, the Red Cross also was able to bring hot lunches to workers cleaning up the mess. Other basic needs were provided for. One dentist realized that people had lost toothbrushes and toothpaste, so she supplied enough for 30 families.

Another response to the tragedy was the large number of volunteers who gave their time. When storm victims came to the centers, volunteers had to be on hand to find what they needed. Donations had to be sorted. Some people spent hours just arranging clothing by size, making it easier to supply the victims with what they needed.

This natural disaster caused suffering for many people. But they have also found that they live in a community that cares. Disaster brought people together.

Circle the signal words that indicate cause and effect in the following sentences.

1. Over 40 families lost their homes because of the 100-mile-an-hour winds.

2. One dentist realized that people had lost toothbrushes and toothpaste, so she supplied enough for 30 families.

3. As a result of the town's involvement, thousands of items of clothing were donated to Red Cross centers.

Answer each of the following questions with a short sentence.

4. What caused damage to the homes of 20 families?

_____

5. What happened because of damaged power lines?

_____

6. Why were volunteers on hand at the center?

_____

7. What was the effect of the local church's effort?

_____

8. Why were some volunteers arranging clothing by size?

_____

9. Read the statements below. If the statement is true, write *T* in the space. If the statement is false, write *F*.

_____ a. Rain destroyed many homes.

_____ b. Rain destroyed many personal items.

_____ c. People not affected by the storm donated their own food and clothing.

_____ d. Many people in Marion went hungry after the tornado.

THINKING SKILL 10. Do you think the positive response of the townspeople toward one another after the tornado was unusual? Explain.

Check your answers on page 68.

Cause and Effect in Paragraphs

When cause-and-effect relationships are explained in full paragraphs, the relationship is not always stated directly. Remember to look for ideas that answer the question of *why*.

Directions: Read the article, then answer the questions that follow.

The Mystery of Sleep

Scientists don't have exact reasons for why we sleep, but they agree that some things contribute to our need for sleep. One reason for sleep is to relax and refresh tired muscles. Another is to allow our brains to rest. Some sleep experts believe that our brains will not work well unless given time off from normal, conscious activity. But we don't sleep the way we do because of the pattern of day and night. We actually have a kind of biological clock. The chemicals in our bodies trigger reactions that make us want to sleep once within a 24-hour period.

Some people can't sleep well no matter how tired they are. People who suffer from insomnia, or sleeplessness, are called insomniacs. They have trouble falling asleep, or they wake up every few hours night after night. Often they also have trouble getting back to sleep. So they are usually tired during the day. The quality of their work often goes down. Sometimes their general health gets worse.

Because many Americans experience insomnia, hundreds of products are sold to help people sleep. Sleeping pills are the most common. Then there are head-warmers, knee pillows, and recordings of soft music or gentle ocean waves. There is even a Sleepy Head mask that is supposed to help a person sleep. The list goes on. Some products are stranger than others and many are quite expensive.

There are many good reasons to stay awake. But it seems that for the sake of both our bodies and our wallets, we should try to get a good night's sleep.

---

1. Why do people want to sleep once during every 24-hour period?

_____

2. Which of the following are suggested as causes for the need to sleep? Put a check next to each cause. **You may choose more than one.**

      a. People have been doing it too long to change.

      b. The brain and body need to relax.

      c. The pattern of day and night makes us sleep.

      d. Our bodies have a biological clock.

      e. Tired muscles need to be refreshed.

3. Which of the following are suggested as effects of insomnia? Put a check next to each effect. **You may choose more than one.**

      a. The quality of a person's work improves.

      b. A person's general health gets worse.

      c. A person wakes up every few hours night after night.

      d. A person feels refreshed in the morning.

      e. A person feels tired during the day.

4. Why are there so many sleep aids on the market in America?

_____

_____

5. What is the most unusual sleep aid mentioned in the article?

_____

_____

THINKING SKILL   **6.** Apparently the pattern of day and night does not really have an effect on our sleeping habits. What type of work schedule supports this conclusion?

Check your answers on page 68.

Comparison and Contrast in a Passage _____

Some ideas are organized by comparison and contrast. When two things are compared, we see how they are alike. When two things are contrasted, we see how they are different.

Directions: Read the passage, then answer the questions that follow.

The Lower-Priced Spread

Margarine was invented because of a contest held by Napoleon III of France. The cost of butter was impossibly high. A prize was offered for a substitute spread people could afford. In 1869, Mege Mouries won the competition with a mixture of skim milk and beef oleo oil. The product was called oleomargarine.

Margarine came to the United Stated in 1874. Dairy farmers were forced to compete with oleo because it was much cheaper than butter. But for a while the price was the only thing appealing about it. At first, the low-priced spread was sold in a lardlike white block and packaged with yellow coloring. Messy mixing was needed to blend in the color. Worried about the competition from oleo, dairy farmers got Congress to place high taxes on colored margarine to discourage manufacturers and retailers from buying or selling it. Sometimes it was the housewife who was discouraged. Margarine seemed difficult to use. The low price was not always worth the time and effort.

Today margarine is still the main substitute for butter. But manufacturers can no longer point out how cheap it is. Prices vary from less than a dollar to over a dollar and a half a pound. In fact, some margarines are the same price as butter! The selling point now is that some margarines are made with vegetable oils, which have little saturated fat. Margarine is also more attractive than it used to be. Packages are more convenient. The soft mixtures in plastic tubs or squeeze bottles are easy to use. And it's as yellow or yellower than butter. The French invention has become an accepted part of life in U.S. homes.

---

1. Which title best states the main idea of the passage?

   (1) Margarine vs. Butter

   (2) Modern Foods

   (3) Margarine Then and Now

   (4) To Color or Not to Color

2. Using the information in the passage, fill in the following chart. Then use it to help you answer the remaining questions.

	Early Margarine	Modern Margarine
Price		
Color		
Made from		
Competes with		
Main selling point		
Ease of use		

3. According to the article, in what way is margarine the same today as it was when it was invented?

(1) It looks the same.

(2) It tastes the same.

(3) It costs about the same amount.

(4) It still competes with butter.

4. What was margarine's original selling point?

_____

5. What is margarine's selling point today?

_____

THINKING SKILL **6.** What health benefits might be gained by substituting a margarine, that has little saturated fat, for butter?

Check your answers on pages 68–69.

Sequence—Time Lines

A time line is a diagram of a sequence of events.

Directions: Read the paragraph and study the time line below; then answer the questions that follow.

Eleanor Roosevelt was an important figure in her own right. Some people might be content to be the niece of one president and the wife of another. But this woman was also politically active and worked hard to help society.

Some of the important events in her life are shown on the time line.

---

1. Match the years on the left with the events from the time line. Write the matching letter on each line.

   _____ **(1)** 1884   **a.** She becomes First Lady.

   _____ **(2)** 1933   **b.** Her husband dies.

   _____ **(3)** 1945   **c.** She dies.

   _____ **(4)** 1962   **d.** She is born.

2. How old was Eleanor Roosevelt when she got married?

   _____

3. When did she become active in politics?

   _____

4. What did she do in 1928?

   _____

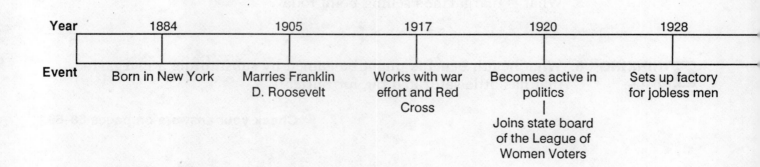

Year	1884	1905	1917	1920	1928
Event	Born in New York	Marries Franklin D. Roosevelt	Works with war effort and Red Cross	Becomes active in politics Joins state board of the League of Women Voters	Sets up factory for jobless men

5. How old was she when she died?

_____

6. Fill in the blanks with the word or words that best complete the sentence.

    a. Eleanor had been married to Franklin for 12 years when she

      began _____.

    b. Eleanor became active in politics in the same year she

      _____

    c. Eleanor was married to Franklin for ____ years.

    d. In 1939, Howard University invited Marian Anderson to sing at Constitution Hall in Washington, D.C. When the Daughters of the American Revolution refused permission because Anderson was

      black, Eleanor protested by publicly _____ from the DAR.

7. Which of the following facts do you learn from the time line? Put a check next to each fact. **You may choose more than one.**

    ____ **a.** Eleanor had five children by the time Franklin came down with polio.

    ____ **b.** Eleanor was involved with at least four organizations.

    ____ **c.** Eleanor's husband became president in 1933.

    ____ **d.** Eleanor took over some of her husband's presidential duties before he died.

T THINKING SKILL

8. Why do you think Eleanor Roosevelt has often been called a role model for modern women even though she was born before women had many political or economic rights?

Check your answers on page 69.

1933	1939	1943	1945	1962
Becomes First Lady of the United States	Resigns from DAR in civil rights protest	Makes Red Cross visits to army bases overseas	Husband dies Appointed to General Assembly of United Nations	Dies in New York

Sequence—Signal Words in a Passage _____

Some words signal the order in which things happen. Examples of such words are *first, second, then, next,* and *after.*

Directions: Read the passage, then answer the questions that follow.

Steps for Fixing a Flat Bicycle Tire

The first thing to do is remove the wheel from the bike. Second, remove the tire. Begin by unscrewing the valve cap and removing any ring on the valve stem. Then deflate the tire. Next use a tire lever to pry a section of the tire over the rim. Leave the lever under the tire. Then free the tire by running a second lever under the rest of the rim. You can now ease the inner tube out and remove the tire.

The third step is finding the leaks. After the tube is out, check the valve for damage. If the valve is good, put a little air in the tube. Now you can check for leaks by putting the tube in water. Bubbles will show the location of any holes. Be sure to mark the hole immediately with colored tape.

Fourth, patch the tire. Wait for the tube to dry before putting the patch on the hole. Rough up the area of the hole with sandpaper. Apply a thin layer of patching cement. Let the cement dry and then smooth the patch on firmly. Fifth, after a few minutes, you can put the tire back on the wheel. Be sure to insert the valve stem first. Otherwise the stem might be crooked. This could cause damage later. Inflate the inner tube slightly. Too much inflation will make it difficult to get the tire on. Tuck the tube gently under the tire and onto the rim. Push the free side of the tire inside the lip of the entire rim.

Sixth, check to be sure that the valve stem is in place and that the tire edges are safely within the rim. Finally, you are now ready to inflate the tire, replace the valve cap, and ride away.

---

1. According to the passage, what is the first step in fixing a flat bicycle tire?

   _____

2. What can be used to make it possible to take out the tire?

_____

3. When do you check the inner tube for leaks?

_____

4. Why should the inner tube be inflated only slightly?

_____

_____

5. The main steps in the sequence are indicated by the words *first, second, third, fourth,* and *fifth.* List six other words that are used in the passage to show the steps in the sequence.

a. _____   **d.** _____

b. _____   **e.** _____

c. _____   **f.** _____

6. Number the following directions in the sequence in which they occurred in the passage. Put *1* next to the first, *2* next to the second, and so on.

_____ **a.** Remove the tire from the wheel.

_____ **b.** Patch the tire.

_____ **c.** Make sure that the tire edges are safely within the rim.

_____ **d.** Put the tire on the wheel.

_____ **e.** Remove the wheel.

_____ **f.** Find the leaks.

_____ **g.** Inflate the tire and replace the valve cap.

THINKING SKILL   **7.** Why do you think that you should check the valve for damage before checking the rest of the tube for leaks?

Check your answers on page 69.

FINDING HIDDEN MEANINGS

TEXT PAGES
95–97

Finding Inferences in a Cartoon

The details in a cartoon help you understand its point. Remember that both the words and pictures are clues.

Directions: Study the cartoon, then answer the questions that follow.

1. What specific detail in the cartoon indicates that it is winter?

_____

2. How does the way the girl is dressed affect her?

_____

3. Why is the woman surprised when she opens the door for the girl?

_____

4. What clues show that the woman is surprised?

_____

5. Where do you think the conversation is taking place?

_____

6. Match the name of each character on the left with her description on the right. Write the matching letter on each line.

_____ **(1)** Elizabeth   **a.** the girl's mother

_____ **(2)** Cheryl   **b.** the girl's friend

_____ **(3)** the woman talking to   **c.** the girl's name
Elizabeth

7. Put a check next to each inference below. **You may choose more than one.**

_____ **a.** The girl didn't borrow mittens or a hat, because they would have made her feel out of style.

_____ **b.** Cheryl lives next door.

_____ **c.** The girl is a teenager.

_____ **d.** The girl doesn't like Cheryl's mother.

_____ **e.** The woman thinks her daughter made the right choice.

_____ **f.** The girl would have been warmer if she had worn mittens and a hat.

8. Based on the girl's last statement, what do you think is the main idea of the cartoon?

_____

_____

9. Based on the mother's expression, write her final response to Elizabeth's reply, "They don't match."

_____

_____

**T THINKING
 SKILL**
10. Does this cartoon accurately describe the way many teenaged girls behave? Why?

Check your answers on pages 69–70.

Finding Inferences in Advertising _____

Advertisers do not usually state directly that they want you to buy their product. The inferences you draw from their ads are intended to make the product appealing to you. Look for stated details and make inferences about how you are expected to react.

Directions: Read the advertisement, then answer the questions that follow.

The Power of Muscles

Tired of sitting home every night? Tired of feeling like a modern-day 98-pound weakling? Now you can change all that. Use Muscles, the cologne for real men. A dab or two of Muscles gives off an aroma of hard work. Even if you sit in an office all day long, Muscles will make you feel as though you spend your time working out in the gym. Women will never ignore you. In fact, they probably won't be able to leave you alone. Other men will respect your aura of strength. The "new you" will be the center of attention.

Why waste time? Be more than just one of the crowd. Become a leader of men today. Wear Muscles!

---

1. This ad is meant to appeal to

   (1) men who work out

   (2) men who feel socially successful

   (3) men who feel socially unsuccessful

   (4) men who like to stay at home

   (5) women who want to date more

2. According to the ad, the kind of men who wear Muscles

   (1) are ignored by women

   (2) work out in a gym

   (3) are physically weak

   (4) want to be leaders of men

   (5) sit at home every night

3. According to the ad, when men wear Muscles they feel like they

   (1) have just worked out

   (2) want to be left alone

   (3) are 98-pound weaklings

   (4) are sweating

   (5) are one of the crowd

4. According to the ad, how do women react to men who wear Muscles?

   (1) Women want to work out at the gym with them.

   (2) Women want to sit at home with them.

   (3) Women are puzzled by their odor.

   (4) Women respect them.

   (5) Women pursue them.

5. Which of the following can you infer from the ad?

   (1) People react negatively to the smell of Muscles.

   (2) Women are attracted to men who wear Muscles.

   (3) This cologne will make men physically stronger.

   (4) Wearing cologne is a waste of time.

   (5) Only women should wear cologne.

6. Which of the following persuasive techniques is best demonstrated by the ad?

   (1) "plain folks" technique—an appeal based on identifying with common ordinary people

   (2) snob appeal technique—an appeal based on a person's desire to be rich or famous

   (3) testimonial technique—an appeal based on a famous spokesperson's support of a product or cause

   (4) bandwagon technique—an appeal to a person's desire to belong to a popular group

   (5) cardstacking technique—an appeal based on focusing only on the favorable points and ignoring unfavorable points

TTHINKING
USKILL   7. According to the ad, in what ways can Muscles change a man's life?

Check your answers on page 70.

Inferences in Literature

You will often have to make inferences when you read literature. Clues to suggested meanings can be found in directly stated ideas. Pay attention to what people do, what they say, and how they say it.

Directions: Read the passage, then answer the questions that follow.

The Question

Driving back, Stiver asked her if she could name all her cousins. She promptly started with Pete's older brother's brood and continued saying names without a pause until she'd named all. "Then, there's my mother's family," she said.

"Someday it would be interesting to trace back your family tree. Ever thought of it?"

"No, but I'll bet you've thought of tracing yours back."

He felt the sting. "Do you know anything about where your family came from?"

"On Dad's side, they come from a little village in Mexico called Trainwreck, for some reason. Mom doesn't know anything except that her folks and their parents were born in Los Angeles."

"Then, you wouldn't say you were from . . . an Early California Spanish family?"

She looked at him evenly. "I'm a Mexican, David. It's not a dirty word. Let me hear you say it." He hesitated. "Go on. Say, 'You're a Mexican.' I want to hear you say it."

He took her hand and looked into her eyes. "You're a very beautiful Mexican girl."

She smiled and relaxed. "Thank you," she said. "I know it's hard for you to say that word, but please don't shy away from it. That hurts most of all."

From *Chicano*
by Richard Vasquez

---

1. What can you infer about the size of the girl's family? Is it small, average, or large?

_____

2. Is Pete the girl's father, brother, or cousin?

_____

3. Where does the girl's father come from?

_____

4. Where does her mother come from?

_____

5. What details are directly stated about the boy and girl during their conversation? Put a check in front of each correct answer. **You may choose more than one.**

_____ **a.** David Stiver wants to know about the girl's family.

_____ **b.** The girl knows why he is asking questions.

_____ **c.** David does not reply right away to the girl's request that he say she is Mexican.

_____ **d.** The girl is tense until David's last statement.

_____ **e.** David thinks the girl is beautiful.

6. Which of the following can you infer about David? Put a check in front of each correct answer. **You may choose more than one.**

_____ **a.** He is from an old Mexican family.

_____ **b.** He is studying family histories.

_____ **c.** He has racial prejudice.

_____ **d.** He thinks Early California Spanish families are better than Mexican families.

_____ **e.** He thinks Mexican families are just as respectable as Early California Spanish families.

7. What can you infer about how the girl feels about being Mexican? Put a check in front of each correct answer. **You may choose more than one.**

_____ **a.** She sometimes feels ashamed.

_____ **b.** She often feels angry.

_____ **c.** She is very proud.

_____ **d.** She is very confused.

_____ **e.** She is aware of prejudice against Mexicans.

THINKING SKILL

8. How do you think David really feels about the fact that the girl is Mexican? Why?

Check your answers on page 70.

Using Inference to Make Predictions _____

Sometimes you need to make inferences before you can predict what is going to happen in what you are reading. You can use directly stated information to make your inferences. Then predict from what you have inferred.

Directions: Read the passage, then answer the questions that follow.

An Important Accident

Many of the world's most important inventions were discovered by accident. Teflon was the accidental result of a scientific experiment.

Teflon was invented in 1938 when Dr. Roy J. Plunkett opened a tank of gas in his laboratory. It was supposed to contain an experimental refrigerant. He was surprised to find the tank was empty. So he split the tank open to find out what was wrong. What he found was a white, waxy powder. Because of his training, he realized that a special chemical reaction had occurred. The powder was very tough and could be turned into a durable coating that material would not stick to.

The first use for this new material was in World War II. Later it was used to line frying pans and cooking pots. But Plunkett is most proud of his accident because of what it eventually contributed to medical and space technology. He had not known at the time that what he had named Teflon would be one of the few artificial materials the body would accept. It can be made into pacemakers, artificial bones, and dentures. Teflon is also so strong that it can resist intense radiation from the sun.

People are always looking for new ways to do things. Sometimes they find things they do not expect. Perhaps because of the kind of accident that happened to Roy Plunkett, cures for cancer or safer ways to produce electricity may be found in the future. Human curiosity can work wonders.

---

1. Which of the following can you infer about Dr. Plunkett?

   (1) He was trying to discover Teflon.

   (2) He was trained as a chemist.

   (3) He disliked science.

   (4) He wanted to name his discovery after himself.

   (5) He was disappointed by what he found in the tank.

2. Fill in the blanks with the word that best completes each sentence.

   a. The passage directly states that Plunkett made his discovery in a

   _____.

   b. Dr. Plunkett was able to recognize that a _____ reaction had happened.

   c. Teflon was used to coat pots and pans because it prevented

   _____.

   d. You can infer that _____ might be a good material to make space suits from.

   e. Plunkett did not know that Teflon would be one of the few

   _____ materials the body would accept.

3. Which of the following uses do you predict Teflon can be put to? Put a check next to each possible answer. **You may choose more than one.**

   _____ **a.** exploring the universe

   _____ **b.** curing cancer

   _____ **c.** creating electricity

   _____ **d.** uncovering new forms of energy

   _____ **e.** creating other lifesaving materials

4. Based on the information in this passage, which of the following can be predicted? Put a check in front of each possible answer. **You may choose more than one.**

   _____ **a.** No more scientific discoveries will happen by accident.

   _____ **b.** Scientists may discover more uses for Teflon.

   _____ **c.** Teflon will no longer be used for medical purposes.

   _____ **d.** Human curiosity will lead to more accidental discoveries.

   _____ **e.** There is nothing left to be discovered.

T THINKING SKILL 5. Do you think Dr. Plunkett could have predicted the many uses for his discovery? Why or why not?

Check your answers on page 70.

More on Using Inference to Make Predictions ____

Directions: Read the passage, then answer the questions that follow.

Sticky Stuff

Over 30 years ago, George deMestral returned home from a walk in the country. As he took off his jacket, he found cockleburs clinging all over it. He had a lot of trouble picking off the burrs. As he got each burr off, he wondered why it stuck. DeMestral closely examined the burrs and his jacket. He found two important features. One was that the burrs had little hooks on their ends. The other was that the loops of cloth on his jacket had gotten caught on the hooks.

DeMestral figured out how to duplicate nature's way of fastening one thing to another. His discovery was named Velcro. The name came from a combination of the words *velvet* and *crochet*.

Today Velcro is made of a sturdy material, usually a plastic. The hooks and loops make it possible for two strips of the same material to stick firmly together. Television host David Letterman demonstrated this fact by wearing a suit made of Velcro and sticking himself to a Velcro wall. Even though he was having fun with Velcro, what he did illustrated how well it works.

Velcro fasteners open and close easily. But they also hold tightly until they are pulled apart. These are qualities that appeal to parents of small children. Velcro fasteners make it easier for small children to dress themselves. The struggle with shoelaces can be put off for a few years.

But this amazing fastener has many other possible uses. The plastics can withstand temperatures of up to 800 degrees. They are strong enough to be used in spaceships.

---

1. Fill in the blanks with the word or words that best complete each sentence.

    a. George deMestral discovered the principle of Velcro after

    _____ .

    b. The passage states that Velcro duplicates the way

    _____ fasten to cloth.

    c. Velcro fasteners _____ because the hooks catch the loops.

2. Which of the following can you infer from the stated information about Velcro? Put a check in front of each possible answer. **You may choose more than one.**

_____ **a.** It was discovered in a planned scientific experiment.

_____ **b.** It is an unimportant invention.

_____ **c.** It is thought of as just a joke.

_____ **d.** It is an accidental discovery.

_____ **e.** It is modeled after cockleburs and cloth.

3. Which of the following can you infer from the fact that Velcro can be used in spaceships? Put a check in front of each possible answer. **You may choose more than one.**

_____ **a.** Velcro holds securely even when there is no gravity.

_____ **b.** Velcro can be called a space-age material.

_____ **c.** Children would be safe in space.

_____ **d.** Space vessels have Velcro walls.

_____ **e.** Velcro is the only material used to make astronauts' suits.

4. Which of the following is a logical prediction? Put a check in front of each possible answer. **You may choose more than one.**

_____ **a.** Children will never learn how to tie their shoes.

_____ **b.** Mothers and fathers won't have to spend as much time dressing their children.

_____ **c.** Mothers will buy more clothing for their children.

_____ **d.** Children will prefer shoes with Velcro over shoes they have to tie.

_____ **e.** Shoelace manufacturers will go out of business.

T THINKING SKILL 5. Do you predict that Velcro will be used more or less in the future? Give one or two reasons for your answer.

Check your answers on pages 70–71.

READING LITERATURE

TEXT PAGES 128–135

Understanding Setting and Character Description

Descriptions of places and people help you to create mental pictures. Details about a place describe a setting. Details about people describe how the person looks and feels.

Directions: Read the passage, then answer the questions that follow.

Part 1: The Meeting

Smoke swirled heavily in the dim light. Jessica tried to make out faces through the haze. Here and there she could pick out heads turned close in conversation. The dull sheen of leather was broken by the glinting sparkle of zippered sleeves and pockets. Puddles on the dark mahogany bar marked the remains of spilled drinks.

Jukebox music muttered softly about an old hippie who can't find a place in the modern world. Well, who can? Jessica thought. She squinted again. For a minute, a familiar pair of rose-tinted glasses reflected back at her. The glasses turned away. He didn't see her leaning against the darkened door.

His long hair was even grayer than six months ago. The dark blue bandana twisted around his forehead made his bushy beard seem whiter. The worn black T-shirt with the Harley-Davidson logo in bright colors showed that he'd been too long on the road. It pulled tight around the belly he was slapping. The result of eating too much greasy food in too many truck stops too late at night. His laugh floated back to her, rough from too much smoking. Jessica shook her head. Tough guy, indeed!

"Hey, teacher-lady," Chick called as he set two beers on the bar, "the traveler's back!"

"I know. He called from Memphis." Jessica edged through the crowd to Tex. "Saw your bike. Ready to go?" As if he were surprised, the man grabbed her around the waist. "So what are you doin' here, little pumpkin?"

Jess patted his shoulder. "Give it up, Marion," she whispered. "Don't call me silly names. And you know good and well I've got dinner waiting. Anyway, your sister's calling in a bit to find out if that book of poetry reached you in Houston."

"Sure, I'm ready for a good time! See all you guys later!"

---

1. Where does the meeting take place?

   _____

2. What details suggest where the meeting is taking place?

   _____

3. What details suggest the people in this place might be bikers?

   _____

4. Fill in the blanks with the word or words that best complete each sentence.

   a. Tex is probably an older man. His hair is _____ and

   his beard is _____.

   b. Tex has probably gained _____ since Jessica last saw him.

   c. Tex probably earns his living as a _____.

   d. _____ is one of Tex's bad habits.

5. What can you learn about Tex from the clothes he is wearing? Put a check in front of each correct answer. **You may choose more than one.**

   _____ **a.** He shops at expensive clothing stores.

   _____ **b.** He dresses like a biker.

   _____ **c.** He doesn't have much money.

   _____ **d.** He is about to go to a classy restaurant.

   _____ **e.** He doesn't care if his clothes are old.

6. Which of the following can you infer Tex wants people to think about Jessica? Put a check in front of each correct answer. **You may choose more than one.**

   _____ **a.** Jessica is a stranger.

   _____ **b.** Jessica is his sister.

   _____ **c.** Jessica is someone he likes.

   _____ **d.** Jessica is a casual girlfriend.

   _____ **e.** Jessica is his best friend.

T THINKING SKILL   7. In what way is Jessica's mention of the poetry book in contrast to the image Tex is trying to present?

Check your answers on page 71.

Understanding the Parts of a Plot _____

A plot is a series of events in a story. The four parts of a plot are the beginning, the conflict, the climax, and the conclusion.

Directions: Read the passage, then answer the questions that follow.

Part 2: The Parting

The low roar of the Harley stopped outside the garage. Jessica opened the back door for Marion.

"Give your ol' Tex a welcome!"

The big man dropped his bedroll to give the woman a crushing hug. He was glad to be at rest. The house was warm and smelled invitingly of hot potatoes, pot roast, and fresh corn.

After dinner, the friends sat on the back porch, watching the red-orange light fade over the Indiana hills. At first, the talk was slow and simple. But later on Maria's telephone call started the old argument. Maria asked her brother the same old question. Marion swore, banged the phone down. When he decided to settle down was his own business! Jessica made the mistake of pointing out that he wasn't as young as he used to be.

"Doesn't it get tiring, keeping your two worlds apart? You could teach again and still ride. No one who knows you would laugh."

"Who asked you, woman?" It was Tex, not Marion, who went into angry sleep on the daybed.

The silence during breakfast was thick. Over the third cup of coffee, Marion (or was it the part of him that Jessica thought of as Tex?) started to talk. He talked about independence. About getting old. About the freedom of the road. And about how good it was to be with someone who didn't judge. Jessica nodded, "So now what?"

"Let's get married."

Jessica spilled her coffee.

"I could keep my bike here. Drive the trucks half the year and spend some time with you. Maybe start writing again. Let's do it."

Jessica took a breath. "Marion . . . Tex . . . make up your mind about who you are. It can't be up to me. No. It's not that easy."

Tex left town early that trip. It might have been the sharp wind that caused the tears as he turned south onto the highway. It might have been the wind that whispered, "It's not that easy, Jessica."

---

1. Does Marion live with Jessica on a full-time basis? How do you know?

_____

2. Why do you think Marion calls himself Tex?

_____

3. Number the following events in the order in which they occur by putting *1*, *2*, *3*, and *4* in the blanks next to the correct event.

_____ **a.** Marion goes to bed angry.

_____ **b.** Marion and Jessica sit on the porch.

_____ **c.** Jessica suggests Marion could teach again.

_____ **d.** Marion and Jessica eat dinner.

4. What caused the argument about Marion settling down?

_____

5. Which of the following best states the conflict in the passage?

   (1) Marion and his sister don't get along.

   (2) Marion must choose between the comforts of home and the freedom of the road.

   (3) Jessica wants Marion to marry her, but he doesn't want to.

   (4) Marion wants Jessica to call him Tex but she won't.

6. Which of the following best states the climax of the passage?

   (1) Maria calls and fights with Marion.

   (2) Jessica spills her coffee.

   (3) Marion explains his plans for their future.

   (4) Jessica refuses Marion's proposal.

7. Why does Jessica refuse Marion's proposal?

   (1) She doesn't love him.

   (2) She doesn't want to marry a biker.

   (3) She is in love with someone else.

   (4) She knows that marriage is not the answer to his problem.

T THINKING SKILL 8. Why is Marion called Tex in the conclusion?

Check your answers on page 71.

Understanding Tone

The tone of a piece of writing tells you how the writer feels. Look for clues that tell you about the writer's emotions.

Directions: Read these diary entries, then answer the questions that follow.

The Long Summer

June 2

Dear Diary,

It happened today! That dumb old man fired me! It made me so mad! He didn't say a word. He had no respect for my hard work during the whole past year. He just had that stiff-faced woman hand me a check and say it was my last day. I've got no words to say how that made me feel and still makes me feel. I said to myself, He doesn't want me to work, and I won't! So I just walked out. Then and there. But I'm still burning up about it!

June 15

Dear Diary,

Why me? It's just not fair. I did my best. It shouldn't have been me. If someone was to have been laid off, it should have been that new woman. Just because she took some extra courses doesn't mean she knows anything. I didn't do anything wrong. I was a good office clerk. It's not fair. They'll be sorry!

July 28

Diary,

No work yet. The places I've been all want you to have a high school diploma. The employment office says something'll turn up. Well, what's gonna turn up is that the landlord'll throw us out in a month or so. The unemployment checks aren't enough. What am I gonna tell the kids?

| | August 15 |

Diary,

There's a job training course that places you after you receive your high school diploma. I decided I should go back to school. It won't be bad. In fact, I bet I'll do just fine. You know, it'll be a good thing for the kids, having a mom who showed them she could do it.

1. Which of the following can you infer about how the woman feels in the first and last diary entries? Put a check in front of each correct answer. **You may choose more than one.**

_____ **a.** She is upset because she had no warning of what was to happen.

_____ **b.** She feels her work experience helped her get ahead.

_____ **c.** She feels sorry for her boss.

_____ **d.** She feels happy about making a change.

_____ **e.** She feels she will make her kids proud of her.

2. What probably bothers the woman most? Put a check in front of the best answer.

_____ **a.** Her boss had someone else hand over the check.

_____ **b.** The new woman took her job.

_____ **c.** She can't support her family.

_____ **d.** The government can't help her.

_____ **e.** She only has a high school diploma.

3. Match the date of each diary entry on the left with its description on the right. Write the matching letter on each line.

_____ **(1)** June 2   **a.** whining

_____ **(2)** June 15   **b.** worried

_____ **(3)** July 28   **c.** determined

_____ **(4)** August 15   **d.** angry

THINKING SKILL 4. Summarize how the woman's feelings changed from the first to the last entry in the diary and why you think her feelings changed.

Check your answers on pages 71–72.

Translating Poetry into Everyday Language _____

Poetic language sometimes may be hard to understand. As you read a poem, try to restate in ordinary language what is being said. Sometimes you may have to read the poem several times before you get a sound idea of what is meant.

Directions: Read the poem, then answer the questions that follow.

I, Too, Sing America

I, too, sing America.

I am the darker brother.
They send me to eat in the kitchen
When company comes,
5   But I laugh,
And eat well,
And grow strong.

Tomorrow,
I'll be at the table
10   When company comes.
Nobody'll dare
Say to me,
"Eat in the kitchen,"
Then.

15   Besides,
They'll see how beautiful I am
And be ashamed—

I, too, am America.

by Langston Hughes

---

1. What does the poet mean when he says he is sent "to eat in the kitchen / When company comes" (lines 3–4)?

(1) He is the cook.

(2) The dining-room table is too small for company.

(3) His table manners aren't good enough for company.

(4) The people he works for don't think of him as their equal.

(5) He doesn't like eating with strangers.

2. What does the poet mean by "But I laugh, / And eat well" (lines 5–6)?

(1) He thinks the situation is funny.

(2) The kitchen is a better place to eat.

(3) He is thriving despite not being accepted socially.

(4) He prefers eating in the kitchen.

(5) He likes things the way they are.

3. What does the poet mean by saying "Tomorrow, / I'll be at the table / When company comes" (lines 8–10)?

(1) Sometime in the future, he will take his place as an equal.

(2) He wants to talk to people when he eats.

(3) Guests are expected for dinner the next day.

(4) The people he lives with have already changed their minds about him.

(5) He is planning a dinner party of his own.

4. What does the poet mean by "the darker brother" (line 2)?

_____

5. What group of people does "They" (line 3) refer to?

_____

6. How will people feel when they realize how beautiful he is?

_____

 **7.** Through most of the poem, the poet seems to be speaking about himself. But the first and last lines suggest something else. Is the poet talking about a group of people? If so, what is he saying?

Check your answers on page 72.

Understanding the Format of Drama _____

Plays must be read differently from prose stories. The most important part of dramatic format is the dialogue—what people actually say. You also can learn about what is happening from the stage directions.

Directions: Read the play excerpt, then answer the questions that follow.

OSCAR: There's something wrong with this system, that's what's wrong. I don't think that two single men living alone in a big eight-room apartment should have a cleaner house than my mother.

FELIX (*gets the rest of the dishes, glasses, and coasters from the table*): What are you talking about? I'm just going to put the dishes in the sink. You want me to leave them here all night?

OSCAR (*takes his glass, which FELIX has put on the tray, and crosses to the bar for a refill*): I don't care if you take them to bed with you. You can play Mr. Clean all you want. But don't make me feel guilty.

FELIX (*takes the tray into the kitchen, leaving the swinging door open*): I'm not asking you to do it, Oscar. You don't have to clean up.

OSCAR (*moves up to the door*): That's why you make me feel guilty. You're always in my bathroom hanging up my towels. Whenever I smoke you follow me around with an ashtray. Last night I found you washing the kitchen floor, shaking your head and moaning, "Footprints, footprints!"

(*He paces around the room.*)

FELIX (*comes back to the table with a silent butler. He dumps the ashtrays, then wipes them carefully.*): I didn't say they were yours.

OSCAR (*angrily sits down in the wing chair*): Well, they were mine, damn it. I have feet and they make prints. What do you want me to do, climb across the cabinets?

FELIX: No! I want you to walk on the floor.

OSCAR: I appreciate that! I really do.

FELIX (*crosses to the telephone table and cleans the ashtray there*): I'm just trying to keep the place livable. I didn't realize I irritated you that much.

From *The Odd Couple*
by Neil Simon

---

1. According to the stage directions, where is this scene taking place?

   _____

2. What is Felix doing throughout the conversation?

   _____

3. According to the stage directions, how does Oscar feel right now?

   _____

4. One stage direction reads: "[Felix] comes back to the table with a silent butler. He dumps the ashtrays, then wipes them carefully." Which of the following best defines a "silent butler"?

   (1) a quiet servant

   (2) a dumb waiter

   (3) an embarrassed guest

   (4) a device to collect ashes and crumbs

   (5) a device that answers the doorbell

5. According to the dialogue, which of the following is true about the characters?

   (1) The characters both like a tidy, well-kept apartment.

   (2) The characters get along well.

   (3) Felix doesn't care how the place looks.

   (4) Oscar likes what Felix does.

   (5) Felix is more tidy than Oscar.

6. Which of the following best describes what is happening in this scene?

   (1) The characters are coming to an agreement.

   (2) The characters are having an argument.

   (3) The characters are doing spring cleaning.

   (4) The characters are meeting for the first time.

   (5) The characters are apologizing to each other.

THINKING SKILL 7. Why is the title *The Odd Couple* a good one for this play?

Check your answers on page 72.

THINKING FOR YOURSELF

TEXT PAGES
172–175

Connotations of Words and Sentences _____

Certain words can suggest emotions and attitudes. The ideas and emotions suggested are called connotations. As you look for the connotations, try to decide if the suggestion is positive or negative.

Directions: Read the passages, then answer the questions that follow.

The Watcher 1

Ever since we moved to this neighborhood, we have been under the eagle eye of the nosy ancient female next door. She spends every minute of the morning with her nose pressed to the window. No tiny movement escapes her prying attention. In the afternoons, she ties up all the local phone lines by spreading her boring gossip. She's lived here forever, so she thinks she knows it all. And she tells us in detail. She never has a good word to say about the people here. Even at night she keeps her spyglass out. That old woman probably makes up weird stories about any strange cars that pull into our drive. A burglar wouldn't have a chance here.

The Watcher 2

Ever since we moved to this neighborhood, we have been watched over by the concerned elderly lady next door. She manages to fill the empty hours of the morning by looking out on what happens near her home. She seems to be quite observant. In the afternoons, she shares her small news by giving all of us a call. She has lived here all her life, so she is familiar with all the families. When she feels there is something we should know, she mentions it. Sometimes she feels she should warn us about someone who might be a problem. Even at night, she doesn't seem to be able to rest well. The poor soul probably wishes she could get to meet some of our many visitors. We all feel a little safer knowing someone is paying attention.

---

1. Indicate which of the following words in each pair is positive and which is negative. Put a *P* in front of the positive word and an *N* in front of the negative word.

   ____ **a.** concerned   ____ **c.** prying   ____ **e.** small news

   ____ **b.** nosy   ____ **d.** observant   ____ **f.** gossip

2. What is suggested by "her nose pressed to the window"?

   (1) The woman cannot control her movements.

   (2) The woman makes a point of seeing what goes on outside.

   (3) The window makes her nose feel better.

   (4) The woman's nose is flat.

3. How does the woman described in "The Watcher 1" seem to feel about visitors to her neighbor's home?

   (1) She isn't at all interested.

   (2) She has something good to say about each one.

   (3) She trusts anyone who visits her neighbors.

   (4) She thinks most of them have bad qualities.

4. The connotations of the words affect the tone of a passage. Which word best describes the tone of the narrator, or speaker, in "The Watcher 1."

   (1) sympathetic

   (2) annoyed

   (3) impersonal

5. Which of the following answers best describes the tone of the narrator or speaker in "The Watcher 2."

   (1) sympathetic

   (2) annoyed

   (3) impersonal

T THINKING SKILL   6. The same person is being described in "The Watcher 1" and "The Watcher 2." If you were this woman's neighbor, which idea about her would you rather have? Why?

Check your answers on page 72.

Recognizing Facts and Opinions

Part of critical reading is understanding what is fact and what is opinion. A fact can be proven to be true. An opinion is what a person thinks is true. An opinion may be based on facts, but it cannot be proven.

Directions: Read the review, then answer the questions that follow.

Streetwise

Move over, Spike Lee! A young black filmmaker is on the scene. John Singleton, at 23, wrote and directed *Boyz N the Hood*. His powerful picture of growing up as an African-American male in an urban environment is frightening. Yet it also offers hope.

Singleton's story has no real heroes. Its action is based on ordinary people fighting to stay alive in a world of violence, drugs, and alcohol. Furious Styles is a neighborhood father. He works hard as an investment counselor. But at home, he works to protect his rebellious son, Tre. Tre has two friends who are half-brothers. Ricky is in line for a football scholarship at the University of Southern California. But his half-brother, Doughboy, deals drugs. Doughboy's future is likely to be a life of crime. All three are caught up in the battle of getting through one more day in the 'hood. Their story is a simple but powerful tale.

The tension of the movie is created in part by its brutal background. The streets are ruled by gangs. Burglars and dead bodies are no surprise to the residents. The police seem to be everywhere except at the scene of a crime. The 'hood is not kind to the people who live there. Not all of them will make it to maturity.

Boyz N the Hood is a movie with a message. Its lesson is not a comfortable one. Singleton does not provide any easy solutions to the problems the young men face. He provides no relief from the deadly pressures of the urban jungle. This young director grew up in a neighborhood similar to the one depicted in the film, with similar challenges. His dream of escaping kept him out of major trouble and eventually led to graduation from film school. Now he has returned to document the terrifying details of the modern ghetto. His movie suggests that the only hope for today's youth lies in fighting against the way things are. But there are no guarantees. Singleton implies that the fight cannot be effective unless America as a whole reexamines its priorities.

---

1. Read each of the following sentences. Write *O* in the blank if it is an opinion. Write *F* in the blank if it is a fact.

_____ **a.** John Singleton is a young African-American filmmaker.

_____ **b.** *Boyz N the Hood* is a movie about young men in the ghetto.

_____ **c.** The movie offers some hope.

_____ **d.** The characters are ordinary people.

_____ **e.** Two of the characters are half-brothers.

_____ **f.** The background of the movie is brutal.

_____ **g.** The movie tells a powerful tale.

2. Based on the opinions expressed in the review, how do you think the author feels about the movie? Put a check next to each possible answer. **You may choose more than one.**

_____ **a.** The movie is well worth seeing.

_____ **b.** The movie has too much violence.

_____ **c.** Americans might learn something from the movie.

_____ **d.** The story line is too simple.

_____ **e.** Only young African-Americans will enjoy the movie.

3. Which of the following phrases suggests the author's opinion about the area the film's characters live in? Put a check next to each possible answer. **You may choose more than one.**

_____ **a.** a good neighborhood

_____ **b.** a quiet street

_____ **c.** the urban jungle

_____ **d.** a world of violence

TTHINKING
SKILL   4. Spike Lee is an established African-American film director. He is known for his realistic films about the problems African-Americans face in this country. What do you think the author intended by beginning the review with "Move over, Spike Lee"?

Check your answers on pages 72–73.

Generalizations

Some opinions are stated as if no other point of view is possible. These opinions are called generalizations. Generalizations often can be recognized by key words such as *always, never, no,* and *all.*

Directions: Read the following passages, then answer the questions that follow.

Dear Editor,

Saturday's article discussing the so-called "mommy track" was way off track. I admit to being a business owner who usually avoids placing mothers in management positions. However, this policy stems entirely from solid business concerns and realities, *never* from unthinking discrimination.

All effective managers put their company before everything else. Mothers can never make that commitment, *and they shouldn't.* Family matters constantly distract mothers from their work, childcare responsibilities force mothers to leave work early, and they are chronically absent because of sick children. I am only protecting my employees' interests by giving promotions and management positions to men and childless women instead of mothers. Mothers are more comfortable on the "mommy track," and secretly they're all thankful to remain safely there.

An Understanding Boss

Dear Editor,

I was horrified by last Wednesday's letter from An Understanding Boss. The only interests he's protecting are his own! Women who are qualified to be managers could never be satisfied with something less. If An "Understanding" Boss were intelligent, he'd promote mothers *before* other workers. Mothers make better managers than childless people because they are more understanding, and anyone who manages a household, an outside job, and children can manage an office. Besides, mothers need financial help supporting their children. How does An Understanding Boss expect single mothers to support their families on a secretary's paycheck? Actually, the Understanding Boss takes advantage of all his employees. Anybody who puts their company before everything else is maladjusted, and anyone who demands that commitment from employees is selfish.

Managing Just Fine Without Understanding

---

1. Using the following list of words, change the generalizations below into opinions. Fill in the blanks with the word or words that best complete each sentence.

| that I've met | seem to | I'd think that |
| may be | Most | what I consider |

   a. All effective managers _____ put their company before everything else.

   b. Family matters _____ constantly distract mothers from their work.

   c. Mothers _____ more comfortable on the "mommy track". . .

   d. _____ women who are qualified to be managers could never be satisfied with something less.

   e. _____ anyone who manages a household, an outside job, and children can manage an office.

   f. Anybody who puts their company before everything else is _____ maladjusted.

2. Find and write six key words that show generalizations are being made in both letters to the editor.

   a. _____ **d.** _____

   b. _____ **e.** _____

   c. _____ **f.** _____

3. Both letters sound convincing because

   (1) they are true

   (2) they are backed up with facts

   (3) they are worded as if they are factual

   (4) they can be proven

   (5) they cannot be proven

THINKING SKILL 4. You can find an exception to most of the statements in these letters. Pick one statement from either letter and write an example of a general or specific exception.

Check your answers on page 73.

Plain Folks and Testimonial Techniques

The plain folks technique uses images that appeal to ordinary people. The testimonial technique uses a person or image that the general public is supposed to believe. Authority figures or other famous people are often used as examples of people who use a certain product or believe in a particular cause.

Directions: Read the passage, then answer the questions that follow.

Elect Anita Chavez

We finally can have a real representative! After four years on the city council and four years as mayor, Anita Chavez is running for state senator. Chavez is one of us! She knows our problems. She understands our worries. She's been in our shoes. So she will vote our way. Anita was born in a small town in northern New Mexico. She and her seven brothers and sisters came up the hard way. They all knew the value of hard work and honesty. To get the money for school, Anita worked weekends as an auto mechanic's apprentice. During summers, she put in long, hot hours repairing roads with the highway department. Anita knew the odds were against her, but she fought the hard fight and won! Now she wants to help you do the same. But you have to help her do it. Vote for Anita Chavez for senator!

A Few Words from People Who Know

Mrs. Hester Donovan, schoolteacher: I've been a teacher for over 30 years. I've seen a lot of students come and go. To my mind, Anita Chavez was one of the best. She never skipped class. Her grades were always excellent. She ran on the track team, sang in the school choir, and headed the debate team. I'll never forget Anita Chavez. You shouldn't either. Vote for her this month!

Karen Leastmoon, well-known film star: Anita Chavez and I met at college. Together we spent many long nights cramming for exams. After graduation, we stayed close. It was Anita who had faith in my talent. She encouraged me to go to my first audition. She was the one who listened to my fears during my first years in Hollywood. I don't know what I would have done without her support. Anita Chavez has been a dedicated friend. She will be just as dedicated to her work as your senator. Vote for Anita Chavez!

---

1. Is the first paragraph an example of plain folks technique or a testimonial? _____

2. What reason is given for Chavez's understanding of the voters' problems and worries?

_____

3. Do any of the details in the first paragraph tell about how Chavez would vote on specific issues? _____

4. What details tell you about Chavez's qualifications as a politician?

_____

5. The details about Chavez's early years are intended to appeal to

   (1) other politicians
   (2) men only
   (3) ordinary, hardworking people
   (4) wealthy voters
   (5) women only

6. The advertising technique used in the second ad is based on which of the following statements?

   (1) Chavez was a member of the high school track team and the debate team.

   (2) Chavez is endorsed by a schoolteacher and a well-known film star.

   (3) Chavez took her education seriously.

   (4) Chavez is a dedicated friend.

   (5) Chavez sang in the high school choir.

**T THINKING
L SKILL**   7. If Anita Chavez were running for election as your senator, is there anything else you would like to know about her? If so, what?

Check your answers on page 73.

Bandwagon and Snob Appeal Techniques

The bandwagon technique suggests that you can be one of the gang if you act a certain way or buy a particular product. The snob appeal technique suggests that you can be like the rich and famous by using the same products they use.

Directions: Read the passage, then answer the questions that follow.

Introducing Purely Clear!

Commercial 1

The setting is a health club gym. Men and women of various ages and different races are using the gym's machines. They are all in fairly good physical shape. Everyone seems to be enjoying the exercise. Their workout clothes are cut to reveal firm muscles covered with a thin layer of sweat. A good-looking young man in a sweat suit walks in carrying a tray of bottles. He calls out, "Break time for Purely Clear!" Everyone stops exercising and crowds around the young man. They are seen smiling as they drink. They all look and feel refreshed. As the camera focuses on a middle-aged Asian man holding a bottle so that the label can be seen, a cheerful voice can be heard. "Be part of a fit America. Take your water break with a healthy swig of Purely Clear!"

Introducing Purely Clear!

Commercial 2

The setting is a quiet, elegant restaurant. Classical music plays softly in the background. A well-dressed couple in their 30s sit at a linen-covered table. The table is set with candles and a delicate spray of flowers. A formally dressed waiter comes to the table. He offers the man a crystal goblet of water from a silver tray. The man sips the water, shakes his head slightly, and hands the goblet back. In an English accent, the man says, "Dear no, this won't do at all. We must have the best. Do bring us Purely Clear." The music fades as a soft voice whispers, "Purely Clear. For people with taste."

---

1. Commercial 1 suggests that by drinking Purely Clear you can become a part of what special crowd?

_____

2. What details in the first commercial suggest the bandwagon approach is being used?

_____

3. According to Commercial 1, how does drinking Purely Clear make you look and feel?

_____

4. The snob appeal in Commercial 2 is based on which of the following ideas?

   (1) The couple is eating in a restaurant.

   (2) Music is playing in the background.

   (3) The entire scene suggests the upper class.

   (4) Anyone can have this experience.

   (5) The waiter is formally dressed.

5. The way the man in Commercial 2 talks about the water is intended to suggest that he is

   (1) tasting a fine wine

   (2) in a hurry

   (3) environmentally aware

   (4) concerned about cost

   (5) conducting a scientific analysis

6. What do the ads suggest about you if you *don't* drink Purely Clear?

   (1) You aren't healthy.

   (2) Your life is boring.

   (3) You are a conformist.

   (4) You are unfit, poor, and have no taste.

   (5) You don't know how to order water.

THINKING SKILL 7. Does either commercial convince you that you should buy Purely Clear? Why or why not?

Check your answers on page 73.

POST-TEST

A poor farmer named Kasaku dreamed that if he should go to the Gojo Bridge in Kyoto, he would become rich. Immediately he started out for Kyoto and at length arrived there. While he was waiting at the bridge, a man came by and asked him what he was doing. So Kasaku told him about his dream. Then the man said that five days earlier he too had a dream, and in the dream he was told that in the yard of the farmer called Kasaku there was an oak tree, and at the foot of the oak tree money was buried. But he said he did not believe in such a foolish dream, and he advised Kasaku to return to his home without believing in his dreams. Kasaku hastily returned home and dug a hole at the foot of the oak tree. He found an old bottle there, filled with many gold coins, enough to make Kasaku a very rich man.

1. Match the parts of a plot with the events they describe. Write the matching letter on each line.

   _____ **(1)** beginning

   _____ **(2)** conflict

   _____ **(3)** conclusion

   a. Kasaku finds gold coins in his yard.

   b. Kasaku has a dream about becoming wealthy.

   c. Kasaku believes his dream but is told that it will not come true.

2. The man that Kasaku met at the bridge didn't find the gold coins because he

   (1) believed Kasaku was the rightful owner

   (2) dug under the wrong oak tree

   (3) didn't believe in his dream

   (4) didn't want to pay the taxes

   (5) arrived at the bridge too late

3. Which of the following titles best expresses the main idea of this folktale?

(1) Don't Talk to Strangers

(2) Beware of Bridges

(3) Five Days to Riches

(4) Follow Your Dreams

(5) Don't Trust Your Dreams

Questions 4–6 are based on the following cartoon.

Beetle Bailey

4. What detail about the people's clothing suggests that they are in the army? _____

5. Which character trait does the title character, Beetle Bailey, show in this cartoon?

(1) responsible

(2) dedicated

(3) fun-loving

(4) serious

6. Which of the following statements best expresses the main idea of this cartoon?

(1) Louise and Sarge are in love.

(2) Beetle Bailey is getting even.

(3) Beetle Bailey is playing Cupid.

(4) Join the army to find romance.

Questions 7–10 are based on the following passage.

Hi, I'm Maria Esquivel. You probably know my name and face from TV. I play Judge Mendez on the popular soap opera *The Wealthy and Worried*. My background as a corporate lawyer prepared me for the role. But it didn't prepare me for my time-consuming schedule. I don't get into my silver Porsche until 8 or 9 o'clock at night after the day's filming. So I don't have much time to spend fixing gourmet dinners. But my demanding tastes are satisfied because I depend on Fine Dining, the perfect microwave meal. Within minutes I can enjoy a Fine Dining entree with all the variety and flavor I need. Fine Dining belongs on your table, too. Believe me, I'm a good judge of taste.

7. Does the effect of the ad depend on a plain folks technique, a bandwagon technique, snob appeal, or facts about the product?

_____

8. What information does Maria Esquivel give about her career to try to make you believe her testimonial?

_____

_____

9. The words *gourmet* and *entree* suggest the food is

   (1) scarce
   (2) convenient
   (3) inexpensive
   (4) elegant

10. The ad implies that Fine Dining

   (1) is a luxury item that you deserve
   (2) should be eaten only late at night
   (3) is difficult to prepare
   (4) can be bought only in Hollywood
   (5) is good for your health

Inventory

1   Four be the things I am wiser to know:
    Idleness, sorrow, a friend, and a foe.

    Four be the things I'd been better without:
    Love, curiosity, freckles, and doubt.

5   Three be the things I shall never attain:
    Envy, content, and sufficient champagne.

    Three be the things I shall have till I die:
    Laughter and hope and a sock in the eye.

by Dorothy Parker

11. What is meant by "the things I am wiser to know" (line 1)?

    (1) I am very wise.

    (2) I shouldn't have known these things.

    (3) I'm glad I could recognize these things.

    (4) I want to avoid these things.

    (5) I'll never be wise enough to understand these things.

12. What do love, curiosity, freckles, and doubt have in common that the speaker would be "better without" them?

    (1) They are all things people want to have.

    (2) They can all make a person unhappy.

    (3) None of them cause problems in a person's life.

    (4) They are all things only women have to deal with.

13. The phrase "a sock in the eye" (line 8) refers to

    (1) eye problems

    (2) surprises

    (3) anger

    (4) unhappiness

Questions 14–16 are based on the following passage.

Sa'Edi, thought of as one of Iran's leading writers, had many of his writings banned. He was politically active and had to move to the United States. The passage was translated by Robert Campbell from the Farsi language.

Hasani said it to me himself: "Let's go over to my place tonight." I'd never been to their place. He'd never been to mine. What I'm getting at is, we were always too afraid of our fathers. He was a lot more afraid than I was. But that night it was different; Hasani was mad at me. He imagined that I didn't like him anymore, that I wasn't his friend. So we went. Usually we just met each other outside. In the morning I would go to their little shack and give a long-drawn-out whistle that Hasani had taught me. When I whistled, Hasani would grab a can and come out. Instead of saying "Hi," we would fight a little. We would hit each other hard so it hurt. That's how we'd decided to behave, and whenever we met, or whenever we left each other, we would fight like that—unless we were either angry or had tricked each other.

From *Dandil: Stories from Iranian Life*
by Gholam-Hossein Sa'Edi

14. Why was it unusual for the narrator to visit Hasani's house?

_____

15. What do you learn about the characters from the way they are described and how they act?

   (1) They don't like each other.

   (2) They are young boys who are friends.

   (3) They feel equally afraid of their fathers.

   (4) They are wealthy.

16. How would you know when these two people are angry at each other?

_____

Questions 17-20 are based on the following passage.

> One of our reporters talked this week to some of our citizens. She asked people on the street a question. Here are some of their answers.
>
> REPORTER: Last month a bill was proposed in our state to set up a nuclear waste disposal site five miles from our town. How will you vote on this issue? Can you tell me why?
>
> BETTY KOENIG: I'd vote against it. Nuclear waste sites cause cancer in all the children who live nearby and kill all the plants and animals.
>
> SAM LIGHTFOOT: My vote would be no! My wife and I lived near the Beatty, Nevada, waste site until we learned that three of the other sites were closed down in the late 1960s. The Sierra Club reported that radioactive material was leaking into our land and water. We moved then. We'd move again if the site here is approved.
>
> SARA FLANNERY: I don't see anything wrong with it. I guess the scientists who run these things know what they're doing.

17. Which person answers the question with a generalization?

_____

18. Is Sam Lightfoot's explanation of how he would vote made up of facts or opinions?

_____

19. Judging from her answer, do you think Sara Flannery would vote for or against building a nuclear waste disposal site nearby?

_____

20. What effect would a nearby nuclear waste site have on Sam Lightfoot's life?

_____

ALICE: I'm doing a lot for my kids. I don't expect them to pay me back at the other end. (*Gene wanders around, thinking, scuffing the grass.*) I'm sure we could find a full-time housekeeper. He can afford it.

GENE: He'd never agree.

ALICE: It's that or finding a home. (*Gene frowns.*) Sidney's folks like where they are. Also, we might as well face it, his mind's going. Sooner or later, we'll have to think about powers of attorney, perhaps committing him to an institution.

GENE: It's all so ugly.

ALICE: (*smiling*) Yes, my gentle Gene, a lot of life is.

GENE: Now, look, don't go trying to make me out some soft-hearted . . . (*He can't find the word.*) I know life is ugly.

ALICE: Yes, I think you know it. You've lived through a great deal of ugliness. But you work like a Trojan to deny it, to make it not so. (*After a moment, not arguing.*) He kicked me out. He said he never wanted to see me again. He broke mother's heart over that for years. He was mean, unloving. He beat you when you were a kid . . . You've hated and feared him all your adult life . . .

GENE: (*cutting in*) Still he's my father, and a man. And what's happening to him appalls me as a man.

ALICE: We have a practical problem here.

GENE: It's not as simple as all that.

ALICE: To me it is. I don't understand this mystical haze you're casting over it. I'm going to talk to him tomorrow, after the session with the lawyer, about a housekeeper. (*Gene reacts but says nothing.*) Just let me handle it. He can visit us, and we can take turns coming to visit him. Now, I'll do the dirty work. Only when he turns to you, don't give in.

GENE: I can't tell you how ashamed I feel . . . not to say with open arms, "Poppa, come live with me . . . I love you, Poppa, and I want to take care of you" . . . I need to love him. I've always wanted to love him. (*He drops his arms and wanders off.*)

From *I Never Sang for My Father*
by Robert Anderson

21. How does Alice feel about her father?

    (1) respectful

    (2) devoted

    (3) indifferent

    (4) resentful

    (5) loving

22. What problem are Gene and Alice discussing?

    (1) how to find a lawyer for their father

    (2) how to handle their father's money

    (3) how to take care of their father

    (4) what song to sing for their father

    (5) how to tell their father how they feel about him

23. The stage directions and dialogue at the end of the scene indicate that Gene

    (1) feels he and his sister are in agreement about their love for their father

    (2) is happy he and Alice are having this conversation

    (3) has a clear idea about how to handle his father

    (4) feels regretful because he never let his father know that he loved him

    (5) is grateful that Alice is handling the situation

The silence was almost deafening. The ticking of the clock sounded like thunder. Jake shifted in the overstuffed chair, trying to feel a little less uncomfortable. He couldn't go to bed yet, not until he knew Natika had gotten home safely. She had promised that she wouldn't stay until closing time. But he knew she would, and so he worried just as he had worried every night for the past year.

Jake and Natika had thought they had it made. They had fallen in love, married, and worked hard to make a good life. Jake was a medical-lab technician and Natika had become a journey-level carpenter. Life was good.

Nothing had prepared them for the day that their six-year-old daughter, Elsie, was run over by a drunk driver. Their world was suddenly broken. Natika found it harder to go home to what seemed like an empty house. She started going to a local bar after work. After a while, one beer led to another and another. She said each drink helped her forget a little more. She said each beer helped her face coming home to a house that no longer held her little girl.

Jake tried to tell her that drinking wasn't the answer. Natika didn't listen. So Jake waited up and worried every night.

Jake must have fallen asleep because he woke to violent sobbing. Natika was huddled on the floor by the door, rocking back and forth. Between gasps and tears, the story came out. She had almost hit a young teenager on her drunken drive home, almost killed a child in the same way her own had been killed.

The next night, Jake waited for several hours in the car while Natika went to her first Alcoholics Anonymous meeting. He knew he would wait that way many more nights. But he also knew that the wait might help to fix their broken world.

24. Where do you think Jake is at the beginning of the passage?

_____

25. Put an *F* next to each false statement. Put a *T* next to each true statement.

_____ **a.** Jake is concerned about his wife.

_____ **b.** Natika was very upset by her daughter's death.

_____ **c.** Jake insisted that Natika work out her own problems.

26. Which of the following is the climax of the story?

    (1) Jake waited for Natika all night.

    (2) Natika started drinking.

    (3) Natika realized she almost killed someone.

Questions 27–29 are based on the following passage.

Around A.D. 105, a Chinese court official named Ts'ai Lun invented paper. Before that time, all writing was done on one of two basic materials. Vellum and parchment were made from dried animal skins. Papyrus was made from reeds that were beaten flat. Ts'ai Lun discovered that he could make a good writing surface from plant fibers and old rags.

Today, the fibers are first mashed to a pulp and then mixed with water. Then the mix is bleached. Next a sizing agent is added so that ink won't be absorbed. Finally, the pulp is pressed into sheets.

Ts'ai Lun's pulping process changed the way people have kept written records. It would take about 12 whole sheepskins to make the equivalent of a 200-page paperback. Just imagine how thick your favorite mystery novel would be!

27. What is the main difference between what parchment and paper are made of?

_____

_____

28. List in order the five steps for making paper.

    (1) _____

    (2) _____

    (3) _____

    (4) _____

    (5) _____

29. What discovery changed the way books are made?

_____

_____

Questions 30–34 are based on the following passage.

A TV commercial shows a group of people waiting at a bus stop. The camera zooms in on a close-up of an African-American man in a business suit. He is holding a briefcase in one hand and a lunch box in the other. A pleasant voice says, "Join Mayor James Frye on his way to work." The camera pans to a wider shot. Mayor Frye starts chatting with a construction worker who is carrying a lunch box like Frye's. Both are nodding and smiling. The pleasant voice comes on again. "Mayor Frye is fighting air pollution in our city. And he doesn't just talk. He listens. And then he practices what he preaches." The camera focuses on the construction worker. We hear him saying, "I admire the way you are setting an example." A bus pulls up. The people begin to board the bus. Mayor Frye, last in line, turns to wave at the camera. The voice says a little more firmly, "If you're not part of the solution, you're part of the problem. Ride with Mayor Frye for another term."

30. Is what the construction worker says fact or opinion?

_____

31. The viewers are supposed to think that Mayor Frye

(1) is one of them

(2) is a poor politician

(3) represents what they would like to become

(4) doesn't understand pollution problems

(5) used to be a construction worker

32. Which of the following details best supports the plain folks approach? Circle the number of the correct answer.

(1) the business suit

(2) the briefcase

(3) the lunch boxes

(4) the pleasant voice

33. Which of the following techniques is used with the voice-over that says, "If you're not part of the solution, you're part of the problem"?

    (1) snob appeal

    (2) plain folks

    (3) bandwagon

    (4) testimonial

    (5) supporting detail

34. What is the purpose of this ad?

_____

Check your answers on pages 65–66.

POST-TEST EVALUATION CHART

Use the answer key on pages 65–66 to check your answers. Then find the number of each question you missed on this chart and circle it in the Item Numbers column. Then you will know which chapters you might need to review before you move on to Contemporary's *GED Test 4: Literature and the Arts.*

Chapter	Skill	Item Numbers	Number Correct
Understanding What You Read	Main Ideas Details and Supporting Details	3, 6 4, 14, 29	____/5
Organization of Ideas	Cause and Effect Comparison and Contrast Sequence	2, 20 12, 27 28	____/5
Finding Hidden Meanings	Inference Predicting Outcomes	5, 10, 34 16, 19	____/5
Reading Literature	Understanding Setting and Character Plot Tone Poetry Drama	15, 24, 25 1, 26 21 11, 13 22, 23	____/10
Thinking for Yourself	Connotations Facts, Opinions, Generalizations Persuasive Techniques	9 17, 18, 30 7, 8, 31, 32, 33	____/9
		Total Correct	____/34

POST-TEST ANSWER KEY

1. (1) b
   (2) c
   (3) a

2. (3)

3. (4)

4. The people are wearing uniforms that suggest they are in the armed forces. The sergeant's stripes suggest that he is in the army.

5. (3) Bailey copes with being in the army with his sense of humor.

6. (2) Bailey is having fun with his superior officers by "messing with their minds."

7. snob appeal

8. She would like people to believe she is trustworthy because she used to be a lawyer and now plays a judge on TV.

9. (4) elegant

10. (1) The description of Fine Dining suggests it is the kind of fancy food eaten by rich people. The phrase "belongs on your table, too" suggests that you should be able to eat fancy food.

11. (3) Knowing about these things made the speaker's life better.

12. (2)

13. (2) A sock in the eye may lead to an eye problem, but mainly it is a surprise. It is something to wake you up to what is going on.

14. The narrator and Hasani hadn't visited each other before because their fathers would get angry. So this visit is unusual.

15. (2) The pronoun "he" shows that Hasani is a male. The reference to their fathers suggests they are children. The way they act together shows they are friends. Their fighting means they like each other, not that they dislike each other. That Hasani lives in a shack suggests poverty, not wealth.

16. The two probably would not fight if they were angry with each other.

17. Betty Koenig. Her answers are judgments that don't allow for exceptions.

18. Facts. All his statements can be proven.

19. For. Her opinions suggest that she is in favor of the project.

20. Lightfoot and his family would move again.

21. (4) Alice says: "He kicked me out. He said he never wanted to see me again. He broke mother's heart over that for years. He was mean, unloving . . ." These lines show Alice's resentment toward her father.

22. (3) Alice and Gene are trying to figure out how to take care of their father whose mind is beginning to fail. They know that soon he will not be able to take care of himself any longer.

23. (4) Gene feels regretful that he never let his father know that he loved him or offered to have him come and live with him. The stage direction: (*He drops his arms and wanders off* . . .) shows that Gene is upset.

24. in a living room at home

25. a. T
    b. T
    c. F

26. (3) This is the turning point. The rest of the story leads up to it. The conclusion resolves it.

27. Parchment is made of animal skin, and paper is made from plant fiber and old rags.

28. (1) Fibers are mashed to a pulp.
    (2) Fibers are mixed with water.
    (3) The mixture is bleached.
    (4) A sizing agent is added.
    (5) The pulp is pressed into sheets.

29. Ts'ai Lun discovered that he could make a good writing surface from plant fibers and old rags instead of sheepskins.

30. Opinion. The construction worker is saying what he feels.

31. (1) The mayor is a hardworking man just like the people he represents.

32. (3) The lunch boxes help to link the mayor and the worker in the eyes of the viewer

33. (3) bandwagon. The statement suggests that you are part of one group or another. It encourages you to join one group.

34. The purpose of the ad is to get the viewer to reelect Mayor Frye.

ANSWER KEY

UNDERSTANDING WHAT YOU READ

Main Idea and Details
Pages 2-3

1. (4) All the details in the passage relate to this sentence. The other sentences are details.

2. (1)

3. (1) c
   (2) f
   (3) d
   (4) b
   (5) g
   (6) a
   (7) e

Your wording may vary, but your answer should contain the same information.

4. They wanted to avoid an accident in which the animal or crew might get hurt.

Main Ideas in Newspaper Articles
Pages 4-5

1. (1) The article is about how the teacher feels about the press. The other choices are details.

2. (2) The article does not give details about the newspaper reports.

3. (1) d
   (2) h
   (3) g
   (4) e
   (5) b
   (6) a
   (7) f
   (8) c

4. television camera crews and newspaper reporters

5. Lynn Hawk wishes the reporters had respected her privacy by leaving her alone in the hospital and not calling her home so much.

Unstated Main Ideas
Pages 6-7

1. (5) The article tells about the invention of the zipper, how it developed, and how it is used now. The first three choices are details. The fourth choice is not mentioned.

2. (1) e
   (2) g
   (3) a
   (4) f
   (5) b
   (6) d
   (7) c

3. a. useful
   b. movable slide
   c. salesman
   d. popped open
   e. keeps clothes securely closed
   f. fastens pants and dresses in a flash

4. The author means that people should be glad that Mr. Judson invented the zipper so that they can dress quickly.

Main Idea and Supporting Ideas
Pages 8-9

1. To get the best deal for your money when looking for a lawyer, find out about the different types of fees.

2. Choices b, c, and d are supporting ideas. Choice a is part of the introduction of the main idea.

3. (1) b
   (2) a
   (3) c

Your wording may vary, but your answers should contain the same information as in the answers below.

4. If a lawyer works 10 hours for you and charges $75 an hour, your bill will be $750.

5. A lawyer might offer to write up your uncontested divorce for a flat—or set—fee. No matter how many hours are spent on your case, all you pay is the flat fee.

6. When a client will not be able to pay for a case unless the case is won and the client receives damages.

7. Answers will vary. Sample: Be sure to shop around when looking for a lawyer, and get a written agreement about the fee.

Summarizing a Passage
Pages 10–11
1. the writer, Ann

2. in the country

3. Edith

4. just after Halloween

5. a. third
   b. first
   c. second

6. (1) is the best summary of the passage. It gives the main idea and details written in Ann's letter to Edith.

7. (4) This answer suggests that several of the same kinds of things happened all in one day.

8. Edith and Ann are good friends. The tone of the letter is casual. Most people would not write their troubles to a business partner. The first and last paragraphs suggest an ongoing correspondence. So does the salutation at the end of the letter.

ORGANIZATION OF IDEAS

Cause and Effect in Sentences
Pages 12–13
1. because

2. so

3. As a result

Your wording may vary, but your answers should contain the same information as the answers below.
4. The damage was caused by flying bricks, wood, and glass.

5. Because of damaged power lines, many families went without electricity.

6. Volunteers were at the center so that they could help victims who came in.

7. Because the local church lent its kitchen, the Red Cross could serve hot lunches to rescue workers.

8. Volunteers arranged clothing by size so that it would be easier to distribute.

9. a. F
   b. T
   c. T
   d. F

10. Answers will vary. Sample: After disasters have occurred, people have often banded together to help one another.

Cause and Effect in Paragraphs
Pages 14–15
1. Chemicals in the body trigger a reaction that makes people want to sleep once during every 24-hour period.

2. Choices b, d, and e are causes for the need to sleep. The other two are ideas that have been rejected.

3. Choices b, c, and e are effects of insomnia. The other two ideas are not.

4. Because so many Americans suffer from insomnia, there are hundreds of sleep aids sold.

5. The most unusual product is a Sleepy Head mask that is supposed to help a person to sleep.

6. Sample answer: People who work the "graveyard shift" at night sleep during the day. Their bodies adjust to this pattern of sleep.

Comparison and Contrast in a Passage
Pages 16–17
1. (3) This title best states the main idea.

Your wording may vary, but your answers should contain the same information as the answers below.

2.

Early Margarine	Modern Margarine
cheap	varies from under a $1.00 to $1.50/lb
white	yellow
milk and beef oleo oil	vegetable oils
butter	butter
low cost	some made with vegetable oils, that have less saturated fats
difficult	convenient

3. **(4)** This is stated. **(1)** and **(3)** are not true. The taste, **(2)**, is not mentioned.

4. its low cost

5. its benefit to health

6. Margarine with unsaturated fat is better for your health and your heart. The fat in butter can cause high cholesterol.

Sequence—Time Lines
Pages 18-19

1. (1) d
   (2) a
   (3) b
   (4) c

2. 21

3. 1920

4. set up a factory for jobless men

5. 78

6. a. working with the Red Cross
   b. joined the state board of the League of Women Voters
   c. 40
   d. resigning

7. Choices b and c. The first and last answers are true but are not mentioned in the time line.

8. Sample: Eleanor Roosevelt became politically active on her own initiative. She did not stay in her husband's shadow or depend on his fame.

Sequence—Signal Words in a Passage
Pages 20-21

1. Remove the wheel from the bike.

2. any lever

3. after checking the valve

4. Too much inflation will make it difficult to get the tire on.

5. Answers may vary. Here are some sample answers.
   a. begin
   b. then
   c. next
   d. after
   e. now
   f. finally

6. a. 2
   b. 4
   c. 6
   d. 5
   e. 1
   f. 3
   g. 7

Your wording may vary, but your answer should contain the same information as in the answer below.

7. If the valve is damaged, that is probably the source of the leak. Checking the rest of the tube before finding the problem would probably be a waste of time. If the valve is damaged, the entire tube should be replaced.

FINDING HIDDEN MEANINGS

Finding Inferences in a Cartoon
Pages 22-23

1. Winter is indicated by the snow.

2. She is freezing.

3. The woman is surprised when she sees that her daughter was out in the cold in just a sweater.

4. The woman says, "Like **THAT?!**" The punctuation and dark type show she is surprised.

5. The drawing suggests that the mother and daughter are in their living room.

6. (1) c
(2) b
(3) a

7. Choices a, c, and f are inferences. The other choices are not.

8. The girl seems to be more worried about wearing clothes that don't match than about being cold. This is obvious because she doesn't borrow the clothes.

Your wording may vary, but your answers should contain the same information as in the answers below.

9. Elizabeth's mother is shocked at her daughter's lack of common sense. She might say, "So what?", when her daughter says the mittens and hat don't match.

10. Yes. Many teenaged girls dress "in style" as a way of fitting in with their peers.

Finding Inferences in Advertising
Pages 24–25

1. (3) The entire ad supports this answer. None of the other groups would be interested.

2. (4)

3. (1)

4. (5)

5. (2)

6. (4)

7. Your wording may vary. Example: Men who wear Muscles will go from being unpopular to popular just by using this cologne.

Inferences in Literature
Pages 26–27

1. Her family is large. "Continued saying names" implies a long list of names. And the list doesn't even include her mother's family.

2. Pete is her father. His brother's children would be her cousins. She also contrasts Pete's family to her mother's.

3. He comes from a village in Mexico called Trainwreck.

4. Her mother comes from Los Angeles.

5. Choices a, c, d, and e are directly stated. Choice b is implied.

6. Choices c and d. His questions and his hesitation suggest he places a lower value on Mexican families.

7. Choices c and e. The way she looks at David and what she says support these answers.

8. He wishes she were from an Early California Spanish family instead of being Mexican. If he weren't prejudiced, David wouldn't have such a hard time saying the word "Mexican."

Using Inference to Make Predictions
Pages 28–29

1. (2)

2. (1) laboratory
(2) chemical
(3) sticking
(4) Teflon
(5) artificial

3. Choices a and e. Teflon can be used in space technology and probably will be used in other materials for the body. The other answers have nothing to do with Teflon.

4. Choices b and d. The relationship between curiosity and discoveries is both stated and implied. The predictions are based on the idea that people will continue to be curious.

5. Answers to this will vary but they should be supported by facts or implications from the passage. Plunkett probably could not have predicted the many uses of Teflon.

More on Using Inference to Make Predictions
Pages 30–31

1. a. walk in the country
b. cockleburs
c. close tightly

2. Choices d and e. George deMestral was not looking for a new type of fastener when he examined his jacket after the walk. Choices a and b are the opposite of what is suggested. Choice c is not implied.

3. Choices a and b. The other three choices are not inferences that can be made about the use of Velcro in space.

4. Choices b and d. Velcro fasteners would make dressing children faster and easier, so less time would be involved. Choices a, c, and e are not logical predictions.

5. Wording may vary but you should have figured that Teflon will be used more in the future. Example: Velcro can probably be used to fasten many more things than have been thought of so far.

READING LITERATURE

Understanding Setting and Character Description
Pages 32–33

1. at a bar

2. dim light, smoky haze, dark bar, spilled drinks, jukebox music playing

3. leather jackets with lots of zippers, dark blue bandana, T-shirt with Harley-Davidson logo, reference to bikes

4. **a.** gray, white
   b. weight
   c. trucker
   d. Smoking/Drinking

5. Choices b and e. The bandana and T-shirt are not what the average man wears. The worn shirt is probably old. Choices a and d are the opposite of what is suggested. His choice of clothing is not necessarily related to how much money he has.

6. Choices c and d. Tex acts as if he knows Jessica, but is surprised to see her. His last comment is intended to suggest he is going out with her for the evening.

7. Tex acts and dresses the part of a tough biker. But the reference to a poetry book implies that he has an educated and sensitive side.

Understanding the Parts of a Plot
Pages 34–35

1. He is just visiting. This is suggested by the two passages. The two have not seen each other for months. Tex is carrying a bedroll, which suggests he does not live at the house. The two are called friends, not housemates or a couple. He also sleeps on the daybed while at Jessica's house.

2. Tex is the name he uses on the road. A person who is a trucker and a biker probably would not want to be known as Marion.

3. (4), (2), (3), (1). Marion and Jessica eat dinner, and then they sit on the porch. Jessica suggests Marion could teach again. Marion goes to bed angry.

4. Maria, Marion's sister, calls and asks him when he is going to settle down.

5. (2) Marion enjoys parts of home life, but he is afraid of being trapped and unable to have his freedom. He is not sure what he wants.

6. (4) When Jessica refuses Marion's proposal, this is the climax, or turning point. The first three answers lead up to the climax.

7. (4) Jessica seems to understand her friend. She appears to know the conflict he feels and also knows only he can come to terms with it.

8. For now, Marion has chosen to play the role of Tex who lives on the road and is not tied down.

Understanding Tone
Pages 36–37

1. Choices a, d, and e. These are supported by details in the first and last diary entries.

2. Choice c. Not being able to support her family is her major concern. The other things bother her, but not as much. The last choice is not true.

3. (1) d
   (2) a
   (3) b
   (4) c

4. Answers will vary. Example: At first the woman was angry because she had been fired. Then she felt that she had been treated unfairly. As time went on, she started to worry about her family's financial situation. Finally, she decided to do something about the problem by entering a job training course after she got her GED.

Translating Poetry into Everyday Language
Pages 38–39

1. (4) Being sent to the kitchen suggests that he is a servant or social inferior.

2. (3) These lines suggest mental and physical health.

3. (1) "Tomorrow" suggests the future. "I'll be at the table" means being accepted as an equal.

4. an African-American person

5. white Americans

6. White Americans will be ashamed of having treated a worthy man as a lesser person.

7. Yes, the poet is really speaking for all African-Americans. He is saying that they are part of America, just as whites are. Even though African-Americans were not treated equally at the time this poem was written, the poet believed that the situation would be different in the future.

Understanding the Format of Drama
Pages 40–41

1. The scene takes place in a room near the kitchen. The mention of the kitchen and telephone table support this.

2. cleaning up glasses and ashtrays

3. angry

4. (4) According to the context, this is the only answer that makes sense. The silent butler clearly is not a person.

5. (5) Felix spends most of his time cleaning up after Oscar.

6. (2) This is supported by the dialogue.

7. Answers will vary. Example: Felix and Oscar share an apartment, yet they are very different from each other. Felix is tidy and likes to clean. Oscar is sloppy and doesn't like Felix's constant cleaning up.

THINKING FOR YOURSELF

Connotations of Words and Sentences
Pages 42–43

1. a. P
   b. N
   c. N
   d. P
   e. P
   f. N

2. (2) She gets as close as she can to what is going on.

3. (4) The words about how she feels about visitors all have negative connotations.

4. (2)

5. (1)

6. Answers will vary. Example: I would rather feel the way the neighbor does in "The Watcher 2." Otherwise I would always be irritated about my neighbor.

Recognizing Facts and Opinions
Pages 44–45

1. a. F
   b. F
   c. O
   d. O
   e. F
   f. O
   g. O

2. Choices a and c. The other answers are not suggested by the author's opinions.

3. Choices c and d. The author uses both phrases to describe the 'hood. The other two are the opposite of how the neighborhood is described.

4. The author is suggesting that John Singleton has enough talent to become as successful as Spike Lee.

Generalizations
Pages 46–47

1. **a.** that I've met/seem to
   b. seem to
   c. may be
   d. Most/I'd think that
   e. I'd think that
   f. what I consider

2. You are correct if you selected any *six* of the following words: entirely, never, all, everything, constantly, only, anyone, all, anybody

3. (3) Both letters contain statements that sound like facts even though they are opinions.

4. Answer will vary. Example: "Childcare responsibilities force mothers to leave work early." Many women have husbands or babysitters who take care of their children in the afternoons.

Plain Folks and Testimonial Techniques
Pages 48–49

1. It is an example of the plain folks technique.

2. She is "one of us," and has been "in our shoes."

3. No

4. She served on the city council and as mayor.

5. (3) The appeal is too general for the other answers.

6. (2) None of the other statements show that the testimonial technique is used in the ad.

7. Answers will vary. Any answer should refer to a real political issue such as taxes, foreign policy, or national health insurance.

Bandwagon and Snob Appeal Techniques
Pages 50–51

1. the health and fitness crowd

2. The ad presents men and women of various ages and racial groups who look and feel fit.

3. refreshed

4. (3) All details contribute to the image of upper class.

5. (1) He acts as though he were judging a wine. None of the other answers are suggested.

6. (3) According to the ads, we must drink Purely Clear to be "part of fit America" and to be "people with taste."

7. Answers will vary according to opinion. All answers should use examples from the ad as support. Example: No. I don't believe that drinking Purely Clear would make me part of the fitness movement. I would also have to exercise.